Zoo Animals

Giraffe

Patricia Whitehouse

Heinemann Library
Chicago, Illinois

Customer Service 888-454-2279
Visit our website at www.heinemannlibrary.com

Designed by Sue Emerson, Heinemann Library
Printed and bound in the United States by Lake Book Manufacturing, Inc.

07 06 05
10 9 8 7 6 5 4 3

Library of Congress Cataloging-in-Publication Data
Whitehouse, Patricia, 1958-
    Giraffe / Patricia Whitehouse.
        p. cm. — (Zoo animals)
Includes index.
Summary: An introduction to giraffes, including their size, diet and everyday life style, which highlights differences between those in the wild and those living in a zoo habitat.
    ISBN: 1-58810-898-8 (HC), 1-40340-644-8 (Pbk.)
    1. Giraffe—Juvenile literature. [1. Giraffe. 2. Zoo animals.] I. Title.
    QL737.U56 W55 2002
    599.638—dc21

                            2001006874

Acknowledgments
The author and publishers are grateful to the following for permission to reproduce copyright material: Title page, p. 21 Stephen G. Maka/DRK Photo; pp. 4, 22, 24 Michael Fogden/DRK Photo; pp. 5, 11 Chicago Zoological Society/The Brookfield Zoo; pp. 6, 20 Martin Harvey/DRK Photo; p. 7 Joe McDonald/Visuals Unlimited; p. 8 Chuck Dresner/DRK Photo; p. 9 John Daniels/Ardea London LTD.; pp. 10, 14 Stephen J. Krasemann/DRK Photo; p. 12 Thomas Dressler/DRK Photo; p. 13 Kim Fennema/Visuals Unlimited; p. 15 Gerald & Buff Corsi/Visuals Unlimited; p. 16 Lisa Hoffner; p. 17 Karl and Kay Amman/Bruce Coleman Inc.; p. 18 Kenneth W. Fink/Bruce Coleman Inc.; p. 19 Diane Shapiro/Wildlife Conservation Society; p. 23 (col. 1, T-B) Chuck Dresner/DRK Photo, Chicago Zoological Society/The Brookfield Zoo, Jim Schulz/Chicago Zoological Society/The Brookfield Zoo/Heinemann Library; p. 23 (col. 2, T-B) Corbis, David Samuel Robbins/Corbis, Jim Schulz/Chicago Zoological Society/Brookfield Zoo; back cover (L-R) Chuck Dresner/DRK Photo, Thomas Dressler/DRK Photo

Cover photograph by Chuck Dresner/DRK Photo
Photo research by Bill Broyles

Every effort has been made to contact copyright holders of any material reproduced in this book. Any omissions will be rectified in subsequent printings if notice is given to the publisher.

Special thanks to our advisory panel for their help in the preparation of this book:

Eileen Day, Preschool Teacher
Chicago, IL

Ellen Dolmetsch,
Library Media Specialist
Wilmington, DE

Kathleen Gilbert,
Teacher
Round Rock, TX

Sandra Gilbert,
Library Media Specialist
Houston, TX

Angela Leeper,
Educational Consultant
North Carolina Department
of Public Instruction
Raleigh, NC

Pam McDonald, Reading Teacher
Winter Springs, FL

Melinda Murphy,
Library Media Specialist
Houston, TX

We would also like to thank Lee Haines, Assistant Director of Marketing and Public Relations at the Brookfield Zoo in Brookfield, Illinois, for his review of this book.

Some words are shown in bold, **like this.**
You can find them in the picture glossary on page 23.

Contents

What Are Giraffes? 4

What Do Giraffes Look Like? 6

What Do Baby Giraffes Look Like? . . 8

Where Do Giraffes Live? 10

What Do Giraffes Eat? 12

What Do Giraffes Do All Day? 14

How Do Giraffes Sleep? 16

What Sounds Do Giraffes Make? . . . 18

How Are Giraffes Special? 20

Quiz 22

Picture Glossary 23

Note to Parents and Teachers 24

Answers to Quiz 24

Index 24

What Are Giraffes?

Giraffes are **mammals.**

Mammals have hair or fur on their bodies.

In the wild, giraffes live where it is warm all year.

But you can see giraffes at the zoo.

What Do Giraffes Look Like?

neck

Giraffes have very long necks and legs.

Their hair is tan with brown or reddish spots.

Each giraffe's spots look a little different.

What Do Baby Giraffes Look Like?

A baby giraffe looks like its parents, but it is smaller.

A baby giraffe is called a **calf**.

New calves are about as tall as
a person.

Where Do Giraffes Live?

In the wild, some giraffes live in **savannas.**

Tall grasses and trees grow there.

In the zoo, giraffes live in large **enclosures.**

The enclosures have grass and trees, too.

What Do Giraffes Eat?

In the wild, giraffes eat leaves.

They use their long, strong tongues to grab leaves.

At the zoo, giraffes eat leaves and **hay**.

Zookeepers put the giraffes' food up high.

What Do Giraffes Do All Day?

Giraffes spend most of the day eating.

Sometimes, giraffes take turns watching the **calves**.

Then, the other mother giraffes can sleep or eat.

How Do Giraffes Sleep?

Giraffes sometimes sleep lying down.

They only sleep for a few minutes at a time.

Sometimes, giraffes sleep standing up with one eye open.

They do this to watch for dangerous animals, like these lions.

What Sounds Do Giraffes Make?

Giraffes are quiet animals.

They usually do not make noise.

Sometimes, giraffes grunt or snort.

Mother giraffes sometimes whistle to their **calves.**

How Are Giraffes Special?

Giraffes can go for weeks without drinking water.

They can get water from eating leaves.

Giraffes have long necks.

But they have only seven bones in their necks—just like you!

Quiz

Do you remember what these giraffe parts are called?

Look for the answers on page 24.

?

?

?

Picture Glossary

calf
pages 8, 9, 15, 19

mammal
page 4

enclosure
page 11

savanna
page 10

hay
page 13

zookeeper
page 13

Note to Parents and Teachers

Reading for information is an important part of a child's literacy development. Learning begins with a question about something. Help children think of themselves as investigators and researchers by encouraging their questions about the world around them. In this book, the animal is identified as a mammal. A mammal is an animal that is covered with hair or fur and that feeds its young with milk from its body. The symbol for mammal in the picture glossary is a dog nursing its babies. Point out that although the photograph for mammal shows a dog, many other animals are mammals—including humans.

Index

babies 8–9

calves 8, 9, 15, 19

colors 6

enclosures 11

food 12–13, 20

fur 4

grass 10, 11

hair 4, 6

leaves 12, 13, 20

mammals 4

necks 6, 21

savannas 10

sleep 15, 16–17

sounds 18–19

spots 6, 7

tongues 12

water 20

zookeepers 13

Answers to quiz on page 22

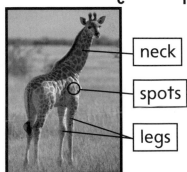

neck

spots

legs

24